The Science Writers' Essay Handbook

How to Craft Compelling True Stories in Any Medium

Michelle Nijhuis

Detail from *Mechanical Painting 6* copyright Mark Chadwick, markchadwick.co.uk. Used with permission.

This project was supported by a generous Idea Grant from The National Association of Science Writers.

ISBN: 0692654666

ISBN-13: 978-0692654668

Introduction

This book is a companion to *The Science Writers' Handbook: Everything You Need To Know To Pitch, Publish, and Prosper in The Digital Age*. If you're looking for advice on getting started as a science writer, on setting up a freelance science-writing business, or on the fundamental skills of idea-finding, reporting, and writing, please check out the *Handbook*.

In this book, I'll discuss how essayists turn ideas into finished essays. I'll talk about essay reporting and research techniques, where and how essays get published, and how essay elements can strengthen many types of stories. I'll look at great science essays old and new, and examine what makes them great.

Though this book is about written essays, its advice is also relevant to photographers, videographers, and radio producers.

This book is intended for college and graduate students, journalists and professional communicators of all varieties and experience levels, and scientists interested in finding a popular audience for their own research. While not all science storytellers are journalists, I believe that all can and should approach their work journalistically—with curiosity, a healthy sense of skepticism, and a sense of responsibility to their readers. No matter who you are, my goal is to help you produce considered, accurate, and compelling essays, even on the tightest of deadlines.

1 | The Art & Science of Science Essays

It lacks the rigor of a laboratory experiment; it does not hold on to its hypotheses long enough to prove them. But it is what it is: a mode of inquiry, another way of getting at the truth.
— Phillip Lopate, *The Art of the Personal Essay*

In 2009, just as a novel strain of influenza began to spread from Mexico to the United States to the rest of the world, writer Eula Biss gave birth to a son in Chicago. Even before a vaccine for the H1N1 flu became widely available, Biss heard other new mothers—mostly affluent, mostly well-educated—debating whether or not to inoculate their children against the virus. Biss had never questioned the value of vaccinations, and she inoculated her son against

1

H1N1 as soon as she could. But she kept thinking about the doubts she'd heard expressed. Where did they come from, she wondered, and why did they persist?

The collection of short essays that Biss published in 2014, *On Immunity*, is not ambivalent. It debunks the supposed dangers of modern vaccines, and makes a strong case for immunization as an obligation to both individual health and the common good. But Biss also points out that history has given us plenty of reasons to distrust public-health measures. When we portray vaccine controversies as either battles between ignorant mothers and educated doctors, or between caring mothers and heartless doctors, we rarely acknowledge that all of the participants are motivated by similar fears and desires. "Rather than imagine a war in which we are ultimately fighting against ourselves," she writes, "perhaps we can accept a world in which we are all irrational rationalists."

I vaccinated my own daughter long before I encountered *On Immunity*. I was appalled by recent news of measles outbreaks driven by vaccine refusals in wealthy communities. Biss, however, both strengthened my commitment and cooled my outrage. I'd read any number of reports on the vaccine "debate," but *On Immunity* helped me understand the ancient, interlocking anxieties beneath it—and by doing so, gave me hope for a resolution.

On Immunity also reinforced my own love and respect for good essays, especially those written by scientists and science writers. Essays allow writers to examine the mind and heart, and speak to both.

They allow science writers, in particular, to go beyond the

simple translation of scientific results in order to engage with science as a human endeavor, one that affects and is affected by our complicated world. They're deeply satisfying to read, and often a pleasure to write.

Before we discuss the process of writing essays, let's get a couple of misconceptions out of the way. Most of us encounter the word "essay" in junior high or high school, when we're assigned five-paragraph compositions that start with a thesis statement, follow it with three paragraphs of supporting arguments, and conclude by more or less restating the thesis. Remember? Maybe you had to write one about the benefits of breakfast, or the causes of the First World War, or symbolism in *The Old Man and The Sea*. These are sometimes called "hamburger essays," because the thesis and conclusion form the bun around the beef.

This book is not about hamburger essays. While the five-paragraph theme is a useful exercise in orderly thinking and writing, it's not really an essay. It's more like a legal argument, in which a foregone conclusion is supported with selected evidence. Good essays have more in common with good science, in that they begin not with a thesis but more tentatively, with a question. ("Why are so many well-educated people afraid of vaccines?") While scientists test their hypotheses through experiments in the laboratory or the field, essayists search for answers through interviewing, reading, and the process of writing and revising. Both scientists and essayists acknowledge that their conclusions are provisional. But by collecting reliable data and thinking clearly and creatively, scientists and essayists alike contribute to a larger, longer conversation.

The other common misconception about essays is that they're musty old things, written with quill pens by men in ruffled collars. Essays do have a long history: Michel de Montaigne, widely acknowledged as the father of the form, published his book *Essais* in 1580. (*Essai*, a word Montaigne coined, comes from the French *essayer*, to try, which in turn comes from the Latin *exagiere*, to sift or weigh out.) Montaigne did, on occasion at least, wear a ruffled collar, and many scholars think the roots of what he called essays reach all the way back to the Greek and Roman philosophers. But Montaigne's confiding voice can sound startlingly modern. "I want to be seen here in my simple, natural, ordinary fashion, without straining or artifice; for it is myself that I portray," he wrote in the introduction to his first collection. Though his subjects range from friendship to cannibals to kidney stones, his voice is always personal—not because he found himself more interesting than other people, but because he felt it would be irresponsible to write from any point of view but his own.

(Note that use of a personal voice doesn't excuse writers from reporting. In fact, it often requires *more* reporting than a just-the-facts "news voice." More on that later.)

The form Montaigne christened, it turns out, is perfectly suited for the digital age. "In this era of prepackaged thought, the essay is the closest thing we have, on paper, to a record of the individual mind at work and at play," writes the critic and essayist Scott Russell Sanders. "Feeling overwhelmed by data, random information, and the flotsam and jetsam of mass culture, we relish the spectacle of a single consciousness making sense of a portion of the chaos." Through the personal voice of an essay, writers can introduce themselves to readers, acknowledge their own biases, and transparently examine complex ideas, providing the analysis and context so valued by modern audiences.

So it's no surprise, really, that essays and essay elements can be found today in features and profiles of all lengths, in most blog posts, in multimedia productions, and even in some forms of social media. Montaigne isn't antiquated; he's everywhere.

A Taxonomy of Essays

The essay is a literary device for saying almost everything about almost anything.
— Aldous Huxley, *Collected Essays*, 1958

The essay form, as the mathematician and science writer Martin Gardner observed, has "irresponsible boundaries." It's so fantastically flexible that it's difficult to pin down. Essays are short, except when they're not; in prose, except when they're not; serious, except when they're tears-in-eyes funny. Though the typical essay in *The New York Times* opinion section ranges from 800 to 1,200 words, essays can be as short as a single image and as long as a book. Long essays can delve deeply into narrow subjects, and short pieces can cover enormous ground: When the neurologist Oliver Sacks learned he was dying of cancer, he wrote "My Own Life," the first in a trio of brief essays that distilled one of the most profound human experiences.

Most scholars distinguish between *personal essays*, which are generally written in the first person and draw from the writer's own experiences, and *critical essays*, which are more often in the third person and respond to a work of art, a scientific advance, an issue in the news, or another current event. Movie reviews are usually critical essays, as are the weekly editorials in the scientific journals *Nature* and *Science*. So, for the most part, is the chapter you're reading now. Both personal and critical essays are written in a personal voice, and use that voice to narrate a journey toward a conclusion.

That brings us to another essential essay ingredient: a journey. Essays are anything but static; the word *essay*, after all, is derived from a verb. The journeys they describe can be emotional, intellectual, physical, or all of the above, but they always start in one place and end up in another. In many cases, as we'll see, the writer's journeys mirror and intersect with the journeys taken by his or her subject. That sense of movement, discovery, and change is fundamental to essays, and it's one of the main reasons that good ones are so satisfying to read.

Many essays, including most of my favorites, have both critical and personal elements. These hybrids are sometimes called familiar essays, a term invented in the early nineteenth century by writer Charles Lamb.

Anne Fadiman, in her essay collection *At Large and At Small*, writes that while critical essays might be said to have more brain than heart, and personal essays to have more heart than brain, familiar essays have equal measures of both:

If I were to turn Lamb's 1821 "Chapter on Ears" into a twenty-first century critical essay, I might write about postmodern audiological imagery in the early works of Barbara Cartland. If I were to write a twenty-first century personal essay, I might tell you about the pimple on my left earlobe that I failed to cover with makeup at my senior prom ... But I don't want to write—or read—either of those essays. I prefer Lamb's original, which is mostly about his musical ineptitude but also about the sounds of harpsichords, pianos, operatic voices, crowded streets, and carpenter's hammers: in other words, about the author but also about the world.

About the author, but also about the world. That's a useful description of any good essay, no matter its species or subspecies.

So essays are written in a personal voice, involve one or more journeys, and are "about the world" in that they are relevant not just to the writer, but also to the reader. That's still a very broad definition. What's *not* an essay?

Polemics are not essays. Neither are their close cousins, diatribes and rants. In fact, as *On Immunity* demonstrates, essays are often a good antidote for polemics. Essays do often express the writer's opinion, but they start with a question, not a foregone conclusion, and they explore the evidence with an open mind. They're rarely neutral, but they are fair.

Straight news stories are not essays. The "news voice," which began to appear in U.S. newspapers in the late 1800s, aspires to have no personality at all. Its job is to deliver the facts as clearly and succinctly as possible, and it still does that job better than any voice we have. "It's a

7

great accomplishment and of enormous importance in our civic life," poet Emily Hiestand says. "News voice and personal voice do different things, and we really need them both."

Feats of "pure narrative" journalism are not essays. Pure narratives are nonfiction pieces where the writer retreats deep into the background, allowing his or her characters to speak for themselves. "Mrs. Kelly's Monster," a 1978 *Baltimore Sun* story about a brain surgeon and his patient by Jon Franklin, won the Pulitzer Prize and is a classic example of pure narrative in science writing. Detailed reporting allowed Franklin to write passages like this one:

> *In downtown Baltimore, on the 12th floor of University Hospital, Edna Kelly's husband tells her goodbye. For 57 years Mrs. Kelly shared her skull with the monster. No more. Today she is frightened but determined.*

Here, Franklin has ceded the stage to his subject. He remains in the wings, directing the action, but the reader, immersed in the real-life experiences and even the thoughts and feelings of the characters, almost forgets about his presence. The narrative tools of fiction—scenes, dialogue, sensory details—are used to give a true story the emotional pull of a novel. (When people say that a piece of nonfiction "reads like a novel," they're usually referring to the effect of these narrative tools.)

Essay writers also use narrative tools, often with wonderful results. But where pure narratives show instead of tell, essays do both, and the best essayists use their distinctive voices to make the telling just as fascinating as the showing. Writer and teacher Phillip Lopate calls such essays "glorious thought excursions," and urges his students not to abandon telling for showing. "What makes me want to keep reading a nonfiction text," he writes, "is the encounter with a surprising, well-stocked mind as it takes on the challenge of the next sentence, paragraph, and thematic problem it has set for itself."

This is not to say that one form is superior to another. Whether your story is best told as a pure narrative, an essay, or as one of the many possible combinations of the two depends on the nature of the tale itself, on your reporting of it, and on your own inclinations as a storyteller.

A Very Brief History of Science Essays

In the first century A.D., centuries before Montaigne wrote his *Essais*, the Roman philosopher Seneca wrote a letter to his friend Lucilius describing a devastating earthquake in Pompeii. "What can anyone believe quite safe if the world itself is shaken, and its most solid parts totter to their fall?" Seneca wonders. There's no escape from this fundamental uncertainty, he reflects, but perhaps comfort can be found in the perspective it provides. "Why should I fear man or beast, bow or lance?" he asks. "Far greater perils are ever lurking for me."

Seneca's letter is an essay in all but name: It's written in a personal voice; it takes an intellectual journey through the events unfolding in Pompeii; and it is not only about the writer but also quite literally "about the world."

I mentioned earlier that good essays have a lot in common with good science, in that both search for answers by sifting through evidence. Seneca, by examining and discarding several possible causes of earthquakes, was acting not only like an essayist, but also like a scientist. (Like many fine essayists and scientists since, he was also wrong: He concluded that earthquakes were caused by pockets of underground air.)

The similarities between the essay and the scientific method spring from a shared history. Both were formalized at about the same time, and both are early examples of Enlightenment thinking. For essayists as for scientists, knowledge depends not on arbitrary authority but on evidence and reason. (Montaigne's catchphrase was "What do *I* know?")

Until the late 1800s, Western scientists routinely shared their results in the form of essays, reporting their journey from hypothesis to conclusion in a personal and often charmingly conversational voice. ("It excited me to a more than ordinary curiosity," Isaac Newton wrote of his famous prism experiment in 1672.) Ada Lovelace's 1843 description of the world-changing potential of the Analytical Engine, a forerunner of the computer, is an extended essay. So is Darwin's *The Origin of Species*, published in 1859.

By the early 1900s, however, the personal voice had disappeared from most scientific discourse, and the passive voice became the norm in scientific reports—perhaps, historians say, because it put the emphasis on the supposedly objective experiment rather than the subjective experimenter. (Personal and partisan voices also faded from U.S. newspapers during this era.) Scientific fields became more specialized, as did their language, and scientists wrote for increasingly exclusive audiences. While some scientists still wrote essays for the general public—*Silent Spring*, by Rachel Carson, was originally published in 1962 as a series of essays in *The New Yorker*—essays were no longer the primary means of communication among scientists.

For most of the twentieth century, in fact, scientists who indulged in any sort of "popular" communication were looked down upon by their peers: Carl Sagan's nomination to the National Academy of Sciences was reportedly rejected by colleagues who disapproved of his television work. Fortunately, more and more scientists recognize that the ability to communicate complicated ideas to general audiences is not a sign of soft-headedness but a valuable, often hard-won skill. As historian Edmund Morgan once observed, "To simplify where you know little is easy. To simplify where you know a great deal requires gifts of a different order: unusual penetration of mind and, above all, sheer nerve."

Today, there are many kinds of science essays, and while some are written by professional scientists, some of the nerviest and most elegant are written by people with little or no formal scientific training.

David Quammen, who writes gorgeous essays on evolution and other scientific topics, studied literature in college, as did Elizabeth Kolbert, who often brings a personal voice to her penetrating reporting on climate change. Bill Bryson, whose subjects range from the history of the Appalachian Trail to the history of the universe, interrupted his college career to travel, returning to graduate with a degree in political science.

In some science essays, the writer draws on research findings as he or she considers a personal experience or observation. In others, the writer contemplates the significance of scientific issues in the news. In still others, the writer shares a firsthand account of scientific discovery and reflects on its implications. Each is about its author, but also about the world.

2 | Finding & Developing Essay Ideas

I had some turning in my head, though I didn't raise my hand.
About nature, mostly, which we were exhorted to reconnect with.
What was it, exactly, and where did it reside?
— Kathleen Jamie, "Pathologies," in *Sightlines*

One of the greatest pleasures—and challenges—of essay writing is that ideas are everywhere. They're in the laboratory and in the field. They're in journal articles, in childhood memories, and in conversations overheard at the coffee shop. Ideas abound; the challenge lies in recognizing them.

Sometimes I think that my most important job as an editor

is to say: "You should write an essay about that." One writer tells me that carpenter bees create perfect circles, something almost no human can do without tools; he should write an essay about that. Another recalls that as a child in Southern California, she believed she could ward off tsunamis by picking up cigarette butts on the beach. Would she *please* write an essay about that?

When I say this, I'm responding to what essayist Kathleen Jamie calls a "turning in my head," a suspicion that the writer I'm talking to will have something to say about the experience or topic just mentioned. I may not know what that something is, and I don't expect the writer to know right away, either. But I'm delighted when he or she tries to find out.

My suspicions aren't always correct, of course. Sometimes a fine writer digs into an enticing tidbit and finds … nothing much, or at least nothing much that he or she wants to say. But I've learned to pay attention to that turning in my head. In this chapter, I'll take a closer look at how it begins.

The Three Ingredients

Why did carpenter bees and tsunamis catch my attention? I don't know much about either, but there are a lot of things I don't know much about, and not all of them are essays in the making. These ideas seemed likely to yield the ingredients essential to all essays: a personal voice, a journey, and relevance to both writer and reader.

I knew that both writers had distinctive ways of expressing their thoughts and feelings on the page. (We'll talk more about developing a personal voice in Chapter 5.) I also knew that their voices were especially suited to their subjects: Stephen Ornes, whose interest in carpenter bees and their circles turned into the essay "Archimedes in the Fence" for *The Last Word on Nothing*, has a gift for putting math in human terms. Heather Abel, who remembered her childhood fear of tsunamis in the essay "How to Stop a Tsunami in Three Easy Steps," also published by *The Last Word on Nothing*, is a talented memoirist.

I also suspected that these ideas could lead to both external and internal journeys. In brief, external journeys— either physical journeys or series of events over time— usually frame an essay's internal journeys, which are its emotional or intellectual "plot." (These journeys are the focus of Chapter 3.) While dramatic external journeys— the birth of a child, the first ascent of a peak—can be useful frames for internal journeys, some of the best essays are inspired by humble experiences, journeys few have taken and fewer have bothered to write about. Neither Abel's childhood walks on the beach nor Ornes' observations of carpenter bees involved outwardly dramatic journeys. But both experiences have the advantage of being particular to the writer, and almost certainly new to the reader.

Both of these stories are also, as Anne Fadiman put it in *At Large and At Small*, "about the world." Abel may have been the only kid who tried to control the ocean by gathering beach trash, but a lot of kids worry about forces beyond their control, and a lot of parents worry about their children's fears. So Abel's account of her internal journey through fear and superstition has very broad relevance.

Ornes' carpenter bees, meanwhile, had reminded him of the story of Archimedes, the Greek mathematician who was so obsessed with making circles that he failed to hear the Roman soldiers at his door. Ornes' internal journey through these two parallel stories is relevant to anyone who's risked their well-being in pursuit of perfection— which is to say, most of us.

The Triggering Question

I wish I could tell you that each time I hear an intriguing idea, I make my orderly and deliberate way through the criteria I've described above. *Personal voice, check! Journeys, check! Broader relevance, check!* The reality is that my vetting process lasts about five seconds, and sounds something like this: "Huh."

When I break down the process as I just did, I can see that, yes, during those five seconds some of my synapses probably do identify the potential for a voice, a journey, and their relevance to the audience I have in mind. But the process is a lot more instinctive, and a lot less rational, than I've made it out to be.

I mentioned in the previous chapter that most essays, like most experiments, start with a question. When I'm considering essay ideas, either as an editor or a writer, it's those unanswered questions—explicit or implicit—that initially draw me in. Abel wondered what to say to modern-day kids who shared her worries about natural disasters. Ornes wondered if carpenter bees were more than just backyard pests. Eula Biss, the author of *On Immunity*, wondered if vaccine controversies really were just battles between ignorant mothers and educated doctors. Interesting questions trigger interesting journeys, and that potential helps start the turning in my head.

In "Pathologies," the essay quoted at the beginning of this chapter, Kathleen Jamie writes of her sudden discomfort with the word "nature." Everyone around her appears to see nature as a benevolent force, an ally, but after witnessing her mother's death, she's not so sure. She writes:

> *I'd felt something at my mother's bedside, almost an animal presence. Death is nature's sad necessity, but what about when it comes for the children? What are vaccinations for, if not to make a formal disconnection from some of these wondrous other species?*

Katy Butler experienced a similar sense of alienation as her father's pacemaker extended his life deep into dementia, placing an agonizing burden on her mother. "Am I weird, or is there something bigger than me going on here?" she remembers asking herself. Through researching and writing "My Father's Broken Heart," a moving essay in *The New York Times Magazine*, she not only explored the emotional trauma her family suffered, but discovered the perverse financial incentives that so painfully delayed her father's death.

Because of the conversational style Montaigne pioneered, these triggering questions often become part of the essay itself. In "A Scientist Dying Young," physicist Alan Lightman writes:

When I recently hit thirty-five myself, I went through the unpleasant but irresistible exercise of summing up my career in physics. By this age, or another few years, the most creative achievements are finished and visible. You've either got the stuff and used it or you haven't. In my own case, as with the majority of my colleagues, I concluded that my work was respectable but not brilliant. Very well. Unfortunately, I now have to decide what to do with the rest of my life.

Lightman's short essay works wonderfully for the usual reasons. It has a personal voice, external journeys (through Lightman's career and the careers of other scientists), and an internal journey through the writer's own notions of success and professional satisfaction. The journeys are, again, both particular and universal: Even if we don't consider ourselves past our prime at 35, we're all aging, and all wondering what to make of the time we have.

I don't think any of that explains why Lightman wrote the essay, though. I suspect he simply wanted an answer to a troublesome question: *What do I do with the rest of my life?*

Sometimes essays lead to answers, or partial answers; sometimes they don't. (Lightman is, if anything, more melancholy about his prospects at the end of the essay than he is at the beginning.) Sometimes they turn up a load of new questions. The satisfaction of a good essay, for both writer and reader, is less in the resolution than in the exploration.

Essays on Demand

Essays inspired by recent events can have deep relevance, too. Often published in the form of columns and blog posts, timely essays can provide what my historian friend April Merleaux calls "emergency context," connecting the news of today with the past and the future. (Higher purpose aside, timely essays are also much easier to publish, and tend to pay more. More on that in Chapter 7.) Writers of emergency context, however, can't sit around waiting for that tantalizing turning in their heads. They need to *make* it happen, on deadline and on topic.

Scientific papers are a reliable source of triggering questions for timely science essays. (See Chapter 2 of *The Science Writers' Handbook* for more about reporting on scientific publications.) New findings may lead you to re-examine your own research or previous reporting. Or they may remind you of a personal experience, beginning the internal journey that will shape your essay. Current headlines are also fertile ground: Abel's tsunami essay was prompted not by a scientific paper but by a *New Yorker* story about the risk of a devastating earthquake in the Pacific Northwest. When that story went viral, Abel recalled her own childhood fears and wondered what to tell her own kids about the news.

Essayists assigned to write about a news item or a scientific discovery can prompt themselves with some all-purpose triggering questions: What needs to be said about this that hasn't been said yet? What have I always wondered about it? What are the most common misunderstandings about this, and why do they persist? (The counterintuitive take— "Everything you know about bacon is wrong!"—has become a cliché in online journalism, but like most clichés it became popular for a good reason: Readers like to be surprised.) Solicit ideas from friends and colleagues, too, especially if you know a lot about the subject at hand. Their questions may help you, as an expert, find a journey that's relevant to your readers.

Journalist and journalism professor Jacqui Banaszynski advises all her students to get in the habit of "curiosity riffing"—to type up all their questions, no matter how silly, about the assignment at hand, and save the unused questions for later inspiration. "Learn to live your life in the form of a question," she says. It's good advice for all journalists, and especially for essayists on deadline.

Nadia Drake, who writes the *No Place Like Home* blog for *National Geographic*, used the New Horizons spacecraft's approach to Pluto in the summer of 2015 as an opportunity to ask herself a triggering question. In her post "Here's the Weird Feature I'd Most Like to See on Pluto," she wrote about her longtime fascination with the mysterious mountain range that runs three-quarters of the way around Saturn's moon Iapetus. In her post, she looked at various theories about the range's formation, considered the chances of a similar equatorial ridge on Pluto, and asked scientists how they would react to the sight of such a ridge. "Our collective brains would just explode," said one.

Personal voice? Check. Internal and external journey? Check. Broader relevance? Check. And while New Horizons did not, in the end, find an equatorial mountain range on Pluto, Drake's readers still took a timely and satisfying trip into a little-known neighborhood of the solar system—in fewer than eight hundred words.

3 | Structuring Essays

Every act of perception is an attempt to impose order, to make sense of a chaotic universe. Storytelling, at one level, is a manifestation of this process.
— John Yorke, *Into the Woods*

Essay writing involves exploration and discovery, and side trips, surprises, and even wrong turns are a big part of the fun. Some wandering in the woods is inevitable. But before you leave home—before you start crafting beautiful sentences, that is—you need to orient yourself on the landscape. Understanding the direction of your journey will save you enormous amounts of time, and leave both you and your readers freer to appreciate the adventure.

The structure of an essay is a lot like the course of a river, writes essayist Paul Graham. Though rivers may appear to meander, they're always flowing downward, carving out the path of least resistance. In a similar way, Graham writes, essays "flow interesting," pursuing answers while wandering in ways unforeseen by both writer and reader. In this chapter, I'll look at how to find and maintain your orientation toward interesting.

One note: I'm addressing essay structure before research not because I think the former should precede the latter, but because research is itself a journey, and many essays are structured around the process. So it's helpful to keep essay structure in mind while you research, and to observe your own journey through interviews and reading.

Start on Tatooine

There is a pattern to the way we tell stories, one that even children follow instinctively, and writers and scholars have described it in a variety of ways. John Yorke, the British screenwriter quoted above, argues that almost every story, from ancient myths to Harry Potter to *Being John Malkovich*, can be divided into three major acts. In the first, the protagonist enters or is thrust into a new world; in the second, the protagonist struggles against an opposing force; in the third, the protagonist integrates old and new.

Or, to put it even more simply, the protagonist goes on a journey and comes back.

I often begin writing classes by pointing out that all stories, and therefore all journeys, have a beginning, a middle, and an end. Students laugh—what could be more obvious?—but when you're in the thick of writing, surrounded by a jumble of facts, emotions, and half-formed ideas, the essential structure of a journey is astonishingly easy to forget.

Let's break down some famous fictional journeys, starting with the original *Star Wars* (Episode IV, geeks). Can you describe Luke Skywalker's external journey in a short sentence? How about his internal journey? Can you identify the beginnings, middles, and ends of these journeys, again in short sentences?

There's no single set of right answers, but here's mine.

External Journey (usually physical): Luke and his companions destroy the Death Star and save the rebellion.

Internal Journey (usually emotional and/or intellectual): Luke begins to discover his identity.

External Beginning, Middle, and End: Luke and his companions escape from Tatooine; they battle evil on the Death Star; they escape from and destroy the Death Star.

Internal Beginning, Middle, and End: Luke commits to a cause outside himself; Luke learns about his Jedi heritage and submits to its discipline; Luke matures into a Jedi warrior.

What about *Charlotte's Web*?

External Journey: Wilbur the pig avoids the butcher, but loses his friend, Charlotte the spider.

Internal Journey: Wilbur learns to care for others.

External Beginning, Middle, and End: Wilbur, forced to leave his comfortable home, faces death; Wilbur, with Charlotte's help, escapes death; Wilbur loses Charlotte, and raises her orphaned offspring.

Internal Beginning, Middle and End: Wilbur is lonely and afraid; Wilbur is befriended by Charlotte and learns to care for her; Wilbur expresses his care for Charlotte by adopting her offspring.

Or *Hamlet?*

External Journey: Hamlet discovers his father's murder and attempts to avenge it.

Internal Journey: Hamlet searches for the will to act.

External Beginning, Middle, and End: Hamlet mourns his father; Hamlet exposes his father's murderer and attempts to avenge his father; Hamlet sets off a household-wide bloodbath.

Internal Beginning, Middle, and End: Hamlet's world is shattered by grief; Hamlet battles and overcomes indecision; Hamlet triggers disaster, but dies knowing he has finally acted.

You get the idea.

This may seem formulaic, and in a sense it is. But it's a formula that has entertained us for literally thousands of years. It can be expanded and contracted, bent and twisted in almost endless ways. It can be left bare, exposed to the reader, or decorated until it's almost unrecognizable. It allows storytellers of all kinds to upend audience expectations without wandering into nonsense. Think of it as a wire frame, a flexible, sturdy guide for both writer and reader.

Most pure nonfiction narratives follow this three-part structure, too: In the first part of "Mrs. Kelly's Monster," the brain surgeon leaves home and enters the operating room; in the second, he approaches and tries to confront "the monster," the knot of abnormal blood vessels in the back of Mrs. Kelly's brain; in the third, he resigns himself to his patient's death.

In most essays, the writer functions as the protagonist, and, as we saw in the last chapter, takes both an internal and an external journey. Those journeys follow a standard three-part structure, but with a twist: In essays, the writer's antagonist is not Darth Vader or the butcher or a murderous stepfather but *an existing story*—either a literal tale or some sort of assumption. Instead of a lightsaber or the One Ring, the protagonist of an essay "comes back" from his or her journey with a new story.

This is most obvious in purely critical essays, where the writer analyzes a constructed story such as a movie or a play. But it's true in every essay I can think of. In "Pathologies," for example, Kathleen Jamie confronts the story that humans are supposed to connect with nature. In "A Scientist Dying Young," Alan Lightman ponders the story that his research career has peaked. In her essay about tsunamis, Heather Abel dispels the story that children react to fear in simple, predictable ways; in his essay about carpenter bees, Stephen Ornes finds mathematical elegance in an insect considered a backyard pest.

Essays, in short, are stories that examine other stories. Where the scientific method tests our stories about the physical world, essays question, complicate, and often overturn our stories about ourselves.

So the first step in orienting almost any essay is for you, the protagonist, to identify the existing story that will serve as your antagonist. Use the Force, Luke.

Consider "The Woman in the Photograph," the prologue to *The Immortal Life of Henrietta Lacks* by Rebecca Skloot.

Existing Story: Henrietta Lacks, the woman whose cells have advanced modern medicine, is doomed to anonymity.

Writer's External Journey: Skloot spends a decade uncovering the story of Lacks' life and the effects of her involuntary "donation" on her descendants.

Writer's Internal Journey: Skloot confronts her own hidden assumptions about science and race.

The members of the Lacks family also undergo external and internal journeys, which have much broader implications than Skloot's personal journeys and rightly dominate both the prologue and the book itself.

But here, as in many essays, the writer's journeys are essential to the *structure* of the prologue. They form the essay's trunk; the other journeys are its branches.

Consider "Superdove on 46th Street," the final installment

in David Quammen's famous "Natural Acts" column in *Outside* magazine.

Existing Story: Pigeons are stupid and helpless.

Writer's External Journey: On a trip to New York City, Quammen notices pigeons.

Writer's Internal Journey: Quammen begins to see pigeons as "superdoves," an example of humans' unwitting transformation of plant and animal species.

Remember what I said about humble external journeys leading to interesting essays? Quammen's external journey consists of three fleeting, unremarkable encounters with city pigeons. But as in "The Woman in the Photograph," the writer's journeys give the essay a subtle but solid structure.

Now let's look at the anatomy of "The Anatomy of Joy," one of Natalie Angier's many columns for *The New York Times'* science section.

Existing Story: Melancholy is worth studying. Happiness is not.

Writer's External Journey: Angier tours recent research on happiness.

Writer's Internal Journey: Angier gains an appreciation for both the difficulty of studying happiness and the importance of it as an emotion.

This is a short essay, less than a thousand words, and written in the third person, not the first. The journeys of both writer and subject are mostly implied, not stated explicitly. But it still has a personal voice (Angier's fanciful vocabulary makes her style one of journalism's most distinctive), journeys that follow a three-part structure, and a clear broader relevance: We've all got a stake in the science of happiness.

The View From the Ceiling

In highly personal essays, where a writer confronts an existing story about himself or herself, it's crucial for the writer to have gained some perspective on the story. Otherwise, as Anne Fadiman might say, the essay ends up with too much heart and too little head. It often takes time to gain this perspective, and it always takes a willingness to see one's own imperfections. "If you are panicked by any examination of your flaws, you will not get very far in the writing of personal essays," writes Phillip Lopate. "You need to be able to see yourself from the ceiling." The most effective personal essay writers cultivate an almost scientific curiosity about themselves and their experiences, dutifully reporting all their observations, flattering and not.

Take "The Empathy Exams," the title essay in a collection by Leslie Jamison. This is a long, complex essay that follows the journeys of multiple characters, some of them imaginary. It moves through disparate places and back and forth through time. Though it is anything but formulaic, it is still structured around the very personal journeys at its heart: Jamison's external journey through successive surgeries and her internal search for empathy in herself and others. She doesn't spare herself from her examination, writing frankly of her own failure to feel empathy for her brother when he falls ill overseas. But she also treats herself and everyone else she writes about with a certain tolerance: All are struggling with the same very human problem.

Jamison's antagonist—the existing story—is the belief that true empathy can only arise spontaneously, and near the end of her essay she dispatches it with a moment of great insight. "Empathy isn't just something that happens to us—a meteor shower of synapses firing across the brain— it's also a choice we make: to pay attention, to extend ourselves," she writes. We often assume that intentionality is the enemy of love, she observes, but some of the greatest acts of love require effort and exertion. Her coolly compassionate voice, surely developed over time and many drafts, serves to reinforce her point.

Structure in Practice

So how does all this work in the real world, on deadline? Here's how I mapped the structure of a post for the science blog *The Last Word on Nothing.*

The day before I was due to write a post, I heard a news report about a government-sponsored "cormorant cull" near where I live on the Columbia River. Thousands of cormorants were being shot to protect juvenile salmon, which cormorants love to eat.

I'd heard about the cull before, but for the first time I wondered if it was an isolated event. I did a quick Web search, and was surprised to discover that humans have been killing cormorants in the name of fish protection for centuries. Huh. So had these past culls really benefited fish? I had a triggering question, and an existing story to investigate.

Existing Story: People are killing cormorants to protect salmon on the Columbia.

I spent an hour or so reading several articles and book excerpts about cormorants, learning that while cormorants had long been scapegoated as fish killers, there was little evidence that fewer cormorants led to more fish. I also learned that the cormorant cull on the Columbia, in particular, was unlikely to do salmon much good; an unpublished analysis by the U.S. Fish and Wildlife Service, circulated by environmental groups, suggested that juvenile steelhead not eaten by cormorants were likely to be eaten by other predators. Though I'd started out thinking that the cormorant cull was a sad but necessary measure, this analysis made it look much more like a sad and pointless measure, one that might be fueled by a historical grudge.

Writer's External Journey: I sit at my desk and read about cormorants (boring, won't include in essay).

Writer's Internal Journey: I begin to question the Columbia cormorant cull.

Writer's Internal Beginning, Middle, and End: I assume the cull is a sad but necessary action; I learn about the shaky justifications for past and current culls; I question the Columbia cull.

In my brief journey through science and history, I'd discovered a story that was new to me, and that I felt was worth bringing back to readers. Though I wasn't done with my research—I figured I was about three-quarters through—I'd broken the elements of my essay into movable parts, and I was ready to make some basic structural decisions.

Many essays start at or near the intersection of the writer's journey with the existing story, then move into a more or less chronological telling of the writer's journey and the revised story that results. Skloot begins "The Woman in the Photograph" by describing the worn photograph of Henrietta Lacks that hangs on her own wall. "Superdove on 46th Street" starts with a description of the "ordinary enough" New York pigeon that Quammen is beginning to see with new eyes. "It doesn't look like a creature of such menacing superiority; it doesn't look like a conqueror of worlds," he muses. "But lately I have cause to wonder." (We'll talk more about opening lines in Chapter 5.)

Similarly, I decided to start my blog post, "Aristotle's Raven," by describing the cull as it had been reported on the news. I would then tell the story of my internal journey in chronological order. (In general, stick with chronology unless you have a very good reason not to. As Rob Irion, the longtime director of the Science Communication Program at the University of California, Santa Cruz, likes to remind his students, "You're not writing the screenplay for *Memento*.")

The initial map of my post looked like this:

Existing Story: People are killing cormorants on the Columbia to protect fish populations.

Internal Journey Beginning: I hear about this, assume it is a sad but necessary action.

Internal Journey Middle: I learn about the long-standing resentment of cormorants, and the shaky justifications for past and current culls.

Internal Journey End: I question the current cull.

This isn't an exact blueprint of my essay, but it does describe its landscape and my general direction through it, and as such it saved me a lot of trial and error at the keyboard. I often use this kind of rough outline to organize my research, and to experiment during the writing process: If I'm tempted to take a side trip, I try doing so within my outline first.

For a final example, let's map an essay that includes both an external and internal journey by the writer. "Superdove on 46th Street" unfolds like this:

Existing Story: Pigeons are stupid and helpless.

External Journey Beginning: Quammen encounters an unremarkable pigeon in Manhattan.

Internal Journey Beginning: Quammen reads a book about the "superpowers" of feral pigeons, developed during their long association with humans.

External Journey Middle: Quammen visits a modern-day pigeon breeder.

Internal Journey Middle: Quammen learns that feral pigeons, by continuing to interbreed with escaped domestics, are becoming ever more exquisitely adapted to human society.

External Journey End: As he's leaving New York, Quammen sees a final few pigeons.

Internal Journey End: Quammen reflects on the larger meaning of feral pigeons.

In the course of his external and internal journeys, Quammen overturns the existing story about pigeons, replacing the mild-mannered birds of our imagination with a flock of savvy survivalists. And in case we were wondering why we should care, he adds that our unwitting experiment in pigeon improvement is infinitely repeatable: "When the last beasts and the last plants left alive are all just as super as we are," he concludes, "the world will be a crowded and lonely place."

Like the principles of storytelling, the essay-structuring practices in this chapter are intended to be bent, twisted, and adapted to your individual writing process. No matter how you use them, they won't prevent you from getting lost at times—nor should they. But they will help you flow toward interesting.

4 | Essay Reporting & Research

The greatest part of a writer's time is spent in reading, in order to write.
— Samuel Johnson, in James Boswell's *The Life of Samuel Johnson*

Even those who should know better assume that essays require less reporting than standard news and feature stories. This assumption is built into the pay structure of magazines, whose fees for reviews and essays are often less than those for news and features. Part of the problem is the illusion of endless supply: It's easy for editors to find writers willing to recount personal experiences or opine on the latest news for little or no money.

But memorable essays require serious research. To take the

reader on a journey through an unfamiliar place or subject, you have to know the territory yourself, and also know something about what others have seen and heard before you. To show the broader relevance of a personal journey, you may need to interview the people who shared it with you, or reconstruct events through research. To bring home the larger implications of new scientific findings, you need to not only understand those findings but also their scientific and even cultural and historical context. The best essays are often at least as deeply researched as comparable news and feature stories.

Which, unfortunately, means that essays—as a rule—pay less than news and features for a similar or even greater amount of work. The good news is that research is an excellent way to make your essays stand out to both editors and readers—and to build a solid case for a higher fee. (Research can also nudge essays across the very blurry line that divides them from higher-paying feature stories.) And while there's pleasure to be had in all kinds of reporting, I find that essay research takes me to the least expected and most fascinating places, making me a more creative and attentive reporter of all kinds of stories.

In this chapter, I'll look at how research can enrich essays, and talk about essay-specific reporting and research strategies. For more basic advice on research and reporting, please see Chapters 4 and 6 of *The Science Writers' Handbook*.

Research for Detail

Reporters are taught to notice details: to not only write down what their source says, for example, but also pay attention to his or her appearance, mannerisms, and surroundings. Carefully selected details help the reader visualize a story, and even imagine its smells, sounds, and tastes. Those sensory connections, the thinking goes, help the writer hold the reader's attention all the way to the end. For similar reasons, reporters also use a variety of sources to reconstruct scenes they didn't witness. What time of day was it when the fire started? What was the weather like? What was the fire chief doing when she got the first call? Interviews, news and historical accounts, and photographs can all provide the details that help draw a reader in.

Such details—carefully observed, and communicated in fresh language—are even more important to essay writers. "The personal voice is the realm of why and how, and it almost always brings in more description," says poet Emily Hiestand. "And it relies very, very strongly on sensory knowledge. Not just sensory data, but sensory knowledge rather than the sheer accounting of fact."

Consider these lines from Jenny Price's essay "The Passenger Pigeon," from her book *Flight Maps*:

> *For weeks, pigeons glutted the town markets. The colonists broiled and roasted pigeons, stewed them in gravy and jellied them in a calf's-foot broth. They salted the birds away in barrels for the winter. Eventually people would long for feathers and the stench of poultry to lift from the air, but for a while the pigeons provoked spontaneous revelry in the streets.*

Though this passage describes a scene that's more than three centuries old, it stimulates all five senses: The reader sees the markets piled with bird carcasses, smells the cooking meat, tastes the gravy and broth, hears the spontaneous revelry, and even feels the tickle of floating feathers and the creepy texture of "jellied" pigeon.

Essay writers, as a rule, don't show their work as thoroughly as news reporters do. While they may include an occasional quote or attribution, they tend to minimize references in order to create a smoother, more immersive experience for the reader. Price, a trained historian, does list her sources in endnotes, so we know that she gleaned these details from two firsthand reports and at least two vintage cookbooks, collecting tastes and textures along with names and ingredients.

When gathering details in the field, remember to record what you hear, smell, taste, and touch, not just what you see. Record your emotional reactions, too—it's easy to forget your initial impressions, and they're often useful in descriptions. Some writers use photographs or voice recordings to supplement their note-taking. (I often talk into a digital recorder while driving home from a day of reporting.)

Whether or not you're present at the scene, field guides, primary research, and experts are great sources of vivid, scientifically accurate details. This passage from "India's Vanishing Vultures," by Meera Subramanian, a *Virginia Quarterly Review* feature story with essay elements, strengthens its firsthand observations with ornithological detail:

> *There were black hawk-like kites and cawing crows, and a few cinereous vultures, massive black figures with an air of royalty. One landed in a treetop, bending the bough with its weight, and scattering eagles to the lower branches, dwarfing them. I saw the*

slender white wisps of cattle egrets standing inside the remains of a massive rib cage, picking at the leftover flesh. There were drongos with long forked tails and hoopoes with black-tipped fanned crests … A black ibis had its delicate downward-sloping bill buried in an unidentified body part, a thick coagulated substance the color of cabernet. Skeletons were piled fifteen feet high, some but not all of the meat picked clean, awaiting the arrival of bone collectors who will grind them for fertilizer or gelatin.

When an essay is based on personal experiences, journals or photo albums can help verify and add specificity to your memories. Interviews with friends, family members, or others who were present at the time can do the same. (See the end of this chapter for advice on interviewing friends and family, and for handling conflicting recollections.)

Published or recorded interviews, newspapers, and historical accounts can add both detail and dimension, as they did for Rachel Carson in "The Marginal World," from her book *The Edge of the Sea:*

They were horn shells, and when I saw them I had a nostalgic moment when I wished I might see what Audubon saw, a century and more ago. For such little horn shells were the food of the flamingo, once so numerous on this coast, and when I half closed my eyes I could almost imagine a flock of these magnificent flame birds feeding in that cove, filling it with their color.

The contrast between Carson's time on the shore and what she knows about Audubon's makes her experience, and the essay that resulted, vastly more meaningful—and more sobering.

Research for Metaphor

Both scientists and writers know that metaphor is a powerful communication tool, perhaps the most powerful we have. Consider the metaphors contained in a single paragraph from *The Lives of a Cell*, the 1973 classic by pathologist Lewis Thomas:

> *Mitochondria are stable and responsible lodgers, and I choose to trust them. But what of the other little animals, similarly established in my cells, sorting and balancing me, clustering me together? My centrioles, basal bodies, and probably a good many other more obscure tiny beings at work inside my cells ... are as foreign, and as essential, as aphids in anthills. My cells are no longer the pure line entities I was raised with; they are ecosystems more complex than Jamaica Bay.*

For Thomas, mitochondria are "responsible lodgers"; other organelles are "little animals," "tiny beings," and "aphids in anthills"; cells are "ecosystems" that are "more complex than Jamaica Bay." Like any good descriptive language, such metaphors and similes help the reader understand the subject at hand, and they form a sensory connection between the reader and the text. Metaphors can also set a mood: When David Foster Wallace, in his *Harper's* essay "Ticket to the Fair," compares horses' faces to coffins and feedbags to gas masks, his readers know they're not on a joyride.

Metaphors have another, deeper function. When we create or read a metaphor, writes author and teacher Carol Bly, "we are deliberately allowing the brain to do what it seriously loves to do. It likes to make connections, and it feels deeper emotions when it makes connections than when it creates descriptions, no matter how nice or classy the adjective constructions may be." (Brain research suggests that metaphors do, in fact, stimulate emotions more strongly than literal language does.) Metaphors give us an emotional and intellectual jolt, and in that jolt lies much of the pleasure of writing and reading.

Good metaphors, though, require research, or at least a solid store of eclectic knowledge. To write the paragraph above, Lewis Thomas had to be familiar with not only cell anatomy but also aphid behavior and the ecology of Jamaica Bay. Annie Dillard, in her 1982 essay "Total Eclipse," draws from both astronomy and botany:

> *The Crab Nebula, in the constellation Taurus, looks, through binoculars, like a smoke ring. It is a star in the process of exploding. Light from its explosion first reached the earth in 1054; it was a supernova then, and so bright it shone in the daytime. Now it is not so bright, but it is still exploding. It expands at the rate of seventy million miles a day. It is interesting to look through binoculars at something expanding seventy million miles a day. It does not budge. Its apparent size does not increase. Photographs of the Crab Nebula taken fifteen years ago seem identical to photographs of it taken yesterday. Some lichens are similar. Botanists have measured some ordinary lichens twice, at fifty-year intervals, without detecting any growth at all. And yet their cells divide; they live. The small ring of light was like these things—like a ridiculous lichen up in the sky, like a perfectly still explosion 4,200 light-years away: it was interesting, and lovely, and in witless motion, and it had nothing to do with anything.*

Like most essayists, Dillard doesn't routinely show her sources, but we can imagine the work involved. How many conversations, phone calls, and encyclopedia and field-guide consultations lie behind this gorgeous, brain-tickling, doubly metaphorical description of a total eclipse of the sun?

Researching for metaphor can mean writing down metaphors in the field, as they occur to you, or trying out possibilities on family and friends as you write. It can mean suggesting comparisons during interviews, or asking your sources to draw their own. (Some physical scientists are especially good at creating metaphors, and are delighted to supply them if asked.) It can mean tracking down a lot of prosaic facts—how fast does the Crab Nebula expand, anyway?—but it can also mean learning to look at the world with the eyes of a seven-year-old: as a place stuffed with wonders, freed of categories, and full of potential connections.

Research for Insight and Meaning

While research almost always leads to more vivid writing, it has an even more fundamental purpose. In the last chapter, I described how research can help the essay writer—the protagonist—vanquish an existing story and return with a new one. In fact, the writer's journey through the material often becomes the internal journey of the essay. In "The Marginal World," Rachel Carson's perspective on the shore is made possible by her knowledge of Audubon's observations. In "Superdove on 46th Street, " David Quammen's reading of current research and his visit with a pigeon breeder radically alters his view of city pigeons.

From my own essay writing and discussions with other

essay writers, I know these insights don't always come easily. It helps to articulate your triggering question and your existing story before you start your research, and as I mentioned in the last chapter, it helps to keep the demands of structure in mind as you research, observing your own journey through interviews and reading. But even a short essay may lead you to dip into work from multiple fields and multiple eras. It's almost inevitable that you'll hit a few dead ends.

In 2015, my editor at *The New Yorker*'s Elements blog asked me to critique a "manifesto" released by an environmental think tank. While the manifesto's content was not particularly new or controversial, it had provoked a heated reaction from the environmental community. It took me multiple phone interviews (almost none of which were quoted in the final piece) and several days of reading and thinking to realize that what was bothering people was not so much the content of the document as its form and tone. Five minutes on Google turned up a literature professor at Penn State who specialized in the study of manifestos, and her reading of the document led me to the insight that would end my internal journey: Manifestos, in general, don't begin discussions but unilaterally end them. By expressing its views in the form of a manifesto, the think tank had rhetorically walked away from a diverse and decades-long conversation.

So while you want to be as purposeful about your research as possible, you also want to be patient, and stay curious. When you do reach a dead end, don't discard what you find; it may lead you to new questions—and new essays.

Organizing Your Research

If you're coming to essay writing as a scientist, or as an experienced science writer, you probably have your own methods of keeping your notes and other research materials in order. Most of those can be readily adapted to essay writing. What's important is to maintain a record of where you've been, and a sense of where you're going.

For very long or complicated essay and feature-story projects, I use a database program called DevonThink to organize journal articles, digital clippings from Web pages, and other documents; for simpler projects, I generally keep notes and citations in a single searchable Word document. When I'm writing a short essay on a tight deadline, such as the cormorant post I described in the previous chapter, I often organize my material within my draft outline, taking notes in longhand as I read on the screen. It's crude, but it works: It gives me an overview of what I've found so far, and keeps me from reporting in circles.

A Few Words About Ethics

Essays allow for more experimentation with language than traditional news stories, and their personal voice means that they often involve stories about the writer or people close to the writer. The opportunity to use inventive language and tell personal stories can make essays especially enjoyable to research and write, but it also raises some ethical questions. Below are the basic guidelines I use in my writing and teaching.

Don't make stuff up. In news reporting, where making stuff up is a firing offense, this goes without saying. But some memoirists and other nonfiction writers hold that it's acceptable to fabricate scenes or dialogue in essays and present them as fact, as long as those scenes and dialogue reflect the "emotional truth" of an experience. As an essay writer who's also a journalist, I strongly disagree: I believe that essay writers have a responsibility—to their subjects, to themselves, to the historical record—to get it right.

That means that if an essay is presented as factual, it should be factual. Fact-checking should be a standard part of your research, and even personal memories should be fact-checked as far as possible (more on this below). The essay form does permit uncertainty, so if your memories are hazy, or if you're speculating about the past or future, simply say so: "I remember it this way …" "We'll never know what happened that night, but I imagine that …"

Treat your sources ethically—even if (or especially if) you're related to them. Journalists are careful not to use family and friends as sources, but essay writers often feature them in their writing. I think it's important to treat family and friends much as journalists treat their sources: Make sure they know they're being written about, give them a chance to tell their side of the story, and, with their permission, take notes or record your conversation to ensure that what you say about them in print is factually accurate.

This process can be as simple as calling up a friend and saying, "Hey, I'm thinking about writing an essay about that time we got lost in the woods. How do you remember what happened?" It may mean using journals, photographs, and interviews with outside sources to check your facts or resolve conflicting recollections. (It may also mean acknowledging the unreliability of memory within your essay: "She remembers that I said ... But what I remember is ...")

In some cases, notifying friends and relatives and listening to their versions of a story may require more complicated or even painful conversations. While you should consider the consequences of your essay for everyone involved (more on this below), remember that your obligation is to accuracy and fairness, not flattery. You're not obligated to please your friends and family—and they're not obligated to be happy about what you write.

Please note: if you have experienced abuse or another crime at the hands of a family member and are writing about the perpetrator, speaking with them before publication may not be advisable or even possible. If you are in this category, pay special attention to the third rule, which is:

Treat yourself ethically. I mentioned at the beginning of this chapter that there is a seemingly endless supply of writers willing to recount personal experiences for little or no money; there's also a seemingly endless public appetite for personal experiences, the worse the better. Laura Bennett at *Slate* argues that this appetite has created a "first-person industrial complex" among digital publications (including *Slate*), which encourages young writers to spill horrific personal stories in hopes of career advancement.

Science writers in particular may be tempted to write about their experiences with mental or physical illness, abuse or addiction. While such essays can be transformative for readers suffering through similar experiences, it's important to consider your motivations for publishing this kind of story, and the possible consequences of doing so.

Don't write a deeply personal essay in order to break into a publication; wait until you're working with an editor and publication you can trust to stand by you through any resulting controversy. Make triple-sure you are on solid legal ground before you publish. (This may mean consulting not only the publication's lawyer but also an independent lawyer with media expertise, especially if there is indemnification language in your contract.) And don't publish until you've considered the short- and long-term effects on you, your family, and your friends, and until you've marshaled the personal support you need to deal with the stress of exposure.

5 | Writing Essays

The hard part of writing isn't the writing; it's the thinking. You can solve most of your writing problems if you stop after every sentence and ask: What does the reader need to know next?
— William Zinsser, *On Writing Well*

We've finally arrived at the alleged subject of this book: Writing!

For writers, complaining about writing is almost part of the job description, but here's a secret: I love it. I can complain about the writing *business* as fervently as any other writer, and *starting* to write is difficult, especially when there are easier, more finite tasks available. (Unwashed dishes and unanswered emails can be surprisingly tempting.) But once I've gotten myself to the keyboard, I really do enjoy the challenge of communicating ideas to readers.

For me, the planning and research I've described in previous chapters make essay-writing easier and more fun. Forethought reduces the frustration I experience in front of the screen, freeing me to play with words and ideas.

There are plenty of books full of good general writing advice. (See Resources & Further Reading.) In this chapter, I'll describe some writing strategies I've found to be especially useful for science essays.

Find Your Voice

When I was a beginning writer, I didn't understand what other writers meant by "finding a voice." Writers were *writers,* not talkers, I thought, and thank goodness for that.

In a workshop with memoirist Chris Offutt, I finally heard a definition: "Voice is the writer's personality expressed on the page," Offutt said, stretching out his Kentucky drawl.

(Keyboards clicked. A student in the front row raised her hand and said, "You said 'Voice is …' and then I spaced out. Could you repeat what came after that?")

As I've said in previous chapters, personal voice is an essential ingredient in essays, and my experience writing and editing essays has taught me that voice is one of a writer's most important assets. Voice can draw a reader in as surely—in some cases more surely—than a sexy subject or a dramatic problem. In science writing, voice can succeed where everything else fails, carving a clear path through a prickly thicket of information.

Consider the voices in these two examples:

> *I think that a good story is one that says, on many different levels, "We're both human beings, we're in this crazy situation, called life, that we don't really understand. Could we put our heads together and confer about it a little bit, at a very high, non-bullshitty level?"*

> *The goal is to show how some new discovery looks to an interested outsider, writing for interested outsiders, using metaphor instead of mathematics. I want the reader to feel that we are both on the same side—outsiders seeking a foothold on the slippery granite face of a new idea.*

The first passage is from an *Atlantic* interview with the short-story writer George Saunders, and the second is from "Inside the Black Box," an essay by the science writer George Johnson. The two Georges make similar points about the role of voice in writing, but they use very different voices; their different vocabularies, rhythms, and moods express different personalities.

While one voice may appeal to certain audiences better than the other, both voices are distinctive, and that distinctiveness holds readers' attention, delivering ideas and making them stick.

So how do writers get hold of this powerful tool? Science reporters often have to unlearn a generic "news voice" when they begin to write essays. Scientists almost always have to unlearn a generic academic voice.

While there's no single foolproof method for discovering one's personal voice, I find it enormously helpful to imagine my audience as an individual, someone unfamiliar with my subject but intelligent, curious, and—perhaps above all—my equal. (This practice can be especially useful for scientists, who are accustomed to audiences of fellow experts and sometimes overcorrect by talking down to popular audiences.)

Imagine yourself talking to someone in a coffee shop or on the bus, somewhere busy but relatively relaxed. How would you communicate your experiences or ideas? You'd want to be understood, so you'd use words familiar to both of you. You'd use metaphors and analogies to connect your world with your listener's. You'd speak in personal terms, but you wouldn't talk only about yourself. You'd probably say what you had to say in the form of a story. And you'd be considerate of your listener's time, and respectful of his or her smarts.

Sounds familiar, right? These are the habits of everyday conversation, the thousands of tiny decisions we all make about vocabulary, pacing, and attitude. Face to face, many of these choices happen automatically, but on the page, with more time to second-guess ourselves, it's easy to become stiff and self-conscious.

To "find a voice" is to find your way back to your literal voice—your unique voice—and adapt it to the page or screen.

Ben Yagoda, in his illuminating book *The Sound on the Page*, interviews a variety of writers about their early experiments in voice. Many began by imitating writers they admired, only gradually discovering their own voices. Many of Yagoda's interviewees say the process wasn't additive but reductive: By putting aside pretense, or excess, or anxiety, each writer found his or her own way to *just say it*.

"You come to your style by learning what to leave out," poet Billy Collins tells Yagoda. As a young poet, he says, he mimicked the more obtuse style used by many of his heroes. Only when he adopted a simpler vocabulary did he begin "to recognize the sound of my own writing."

I'll add one wrinkle to Offutt's definition above: Voice is the personality the writer *chooses* to express on the page. "In a real essay, you're writing for yourself. You're thinking out loud. But not quite," writes essayist Paul Graham. "Just as inviting people over forces you to clean up your apartment, writing something that other people will read forces you to think well." Your published voice is a polished-up slice of the complex person you are, and you may choose different slices for different subjects and publications. But over time, most writers discover a consistent core style by which they can represent themselves and their ideas to readers.

So. Choose your writing tools, imagine your curious, intelligent, distractible audience, and get comfortable. It's time to exercise your voice.

Write the First Line

One of the advantages of thinking and planning before writing is that you can dodge the dull horror of the blank page or screen. When I'm ready to write, I transfer my notes from the process described in Chapters 3 and 4 into a new document. That not only puts words on the page right away, but also provides me with an outline, roughly dividing both my internal and external journeys into three acts. (Note that these "acts" can be of very different lengths.)

Next, if I have additional notes from interviews or research, I reread them, copying and pasting the most vivid or important material into my outline. Ideally, I move enough material into my working document so that I can write a first draft without referring to my notes. (Some people use Scrivener or similar programs to keep their notes organized and accessible while they write.)

As I mentioned in Chapter 1, essay writers both "show" and "tell," using not only scenes but also their personal voices to guide their readers through the essay's journeys. Research often suggests where to show and where to tell: After I researched my essay about cormorants on the Columbia River, and organized my research within my outline, I knew I had the material to show two very short scenes. I used the first, the ongoing cull at the mouth of the river, as the opening paragraph of the essay. I used the second, the "stompings" of cormorants in the U.S. Midwest, to dramatize humans' visceral and enduring dislike of cormorants. I used my personal voice to tell the rest of the essay.

Your outline should help you decide *where* to start; the next step is to decide *how*. It's not necessary to start writing with the first line—many writers start with scenes from the middle, or by fleshing out the ideas they want to express at the end. I sometimes do this when I'm stymied, but I prefer to write essays from start to finish—I think I'm clearer and more coherent if I force myself to write an essay in the order it will be read. Writing in order is also more efficient: Because so much about an essay is determined by its entry point into an experience or idea, confirming that entry point early on saves time in the revision and editing stage.

As I mentioned in Chapter 3, essays often begin at or near a writer's encounter with the existing story that serves as an "antagonist" during his or her journeys. Though many opening lines suggest that encounter, there are countless ways to do so. Here's a sampling:

The custom of drinking orange juice with breakfast is not very widespread, taking the world as a whole, and is thought by many people to be a distinctly American habit. — John McPhee, *Oranges*

Among mathematicians and theoretical physicists there can be a continuum of behavior that ranges between the profoundly eccentric and the truly mentally disturbed. — Jeremy Bernstein, "Nash," in *The Merely Personal*

Flat head, lidless eyes, body dirt brown, the Surinam toad slithers through the pond like animated mud, an amphibian golem. — Kim Todd, "Curious"

My planet fetish began, as best I can recall, in third grade, at age eight—right around the time I learned that Earth had siblings in space, just as I had older brothers in high school and college. — Dava Sobel, "Model Worlds," in *The Planets*

The first story I ever heard about immunity was told to me by my father, a doctor, when I was very young. — Eula Biss, *On Immunity*

I learned about a lot of things in medical school, but mortality wasn't one of them. — Atul Gawande, "No Risky Chances"

It's May and I've just awakened from a nap, curled against sagebrush the way my dog taught me to sleep—sheltered from wind. — Gretel Ehrlich, "The Solace of Open Spaces"

Four in the morning and I crawl out of the tent, thinking, what's my penis for, anyway, other than pissing? — Charles D'Ambrosio, "Whaling out West," in *Loitering: New and Collected Essays*

Some of these first lines introduce a problem or an argument (about the mental health of mathematicians, or the place of mortality in medical-school curricula, or the variety in global orange consumption by humans). Others situate the writer in time (when I was very young; in May; four in the morning) or place (curled against sagebrush; watching a lizard; crawling out of a tent). Some accomplish multiple tasks.

These lines also tell the reader something about the writer. Is she or he nostalgic, playful, serious, analytical, or all of the above? Is she taciturn or talkative? Is she given to sleeping outdoors? Does he wake up at four in the morning, wondering what his penis is for? The writer may well reveal more about her or himself later in the essay, but opening lines are often used to give the reader a sense of the guide on duty.

Scientists trying their hand at popular essays often mimic

the structure of research papers, stuffing an "introduction" with background information. (News reporters, on the other hand, often rush to summarize their conclusions.) Remember that the readers of your essay are free to hop off the train at any moment. Don't load them down with background before you leave the station, but don't give away everything about your destination in your first line, either. Instead, invite your readers to join a journey that's already gaining momentum.

News and magazine writers will have heard the term "nut graf"—journalese for a paragraph, typically placed near the end of the first section of an essay or feature story, that foreshadows the rest of the piece. Nut grafs are notorious for giving away too much, and they can get extremely formulaic; look for the paragraph that begins "This is a story of …" or "Across the country …" When done right, though, they simply suggest the territory ahead, teasing readers just enough to keep them on the train.

If you've done the thinking and planning suggested in Chapter 3, you should be able to write a nut graf with ease, and doing so is always a good exercise. (If you can't distill the general orientation of your essay into a couple of sentences before you write, you probably need to do more thinking.) But you're not obligated to include a conventional nut graf in your essay, and you're certainly not obligated to put it in its conventional place. To paraphrase the journalist Jacqui Banaszynski, your readers need to know what kind of boots to put on—in other words, they need some sort of mental preparation for the journeys to come. How and where you prepare them is up to you.

Face Your Second Act Problems

The joke has it: remembering you set out to drain the swamp is hard when you're up to your ass in alligators. And that is the problem of the second act.
— David Mamet, *Three Uses of the Knife*

Middles can be hard. In the beginning, you introduced yourself and your journey to the reader, and energetically set off toward your destination. Now, you've got to keep going. "In the middle term," writes the playwright David Mamet, "the high-minded goal has devolved into what seems to be a quotidian, mechanical, and ordinary drudgery."

This, I find, is where the essay form comes to the rescue. In a conventional news or feature story, the middle often feels like a recitation. "Here's all the information not interesting enough to put at the beginning or the end," the writer seems to say with a sigh. When a writer acts like an essayist, though, he or she is breaking trail just a few steps ahead of the reader, using a personal voice to grapple with the questions at hand. No matter how carefully you've mapped out your internal and external journeys, and no matter how thoroughly you've researched your subject, you're sure to discover new things in the process of writing an essay, and this promise can keep both you and your reader moving through the middle—alligators be damned.

If you feel yourself losing momentum, check your balance of showing and telling: A scene can go a long way toward reviving both writer and reader. In the middle of "Galvani," an essay about the eighteenth-century scientist Luigi Galvani, George Johnson pauses to describe an early experiment with frogs:

As clouds gathered to the south, he positioned the headless specimen on a table and connected it to a clothesline of wire, which he had strung overhead. Then he waited for an electrical storm, observing that the legs twitched in response to lightning as though warning of the coming thunder.

This gruesome little scene (which is illustrated by an Edward Gorey-esque engraving from Galvani's original report) provides an external frame for the scientist's subsequent internal journey through electrochemical theory—and jolts the reader as firmly as one of Galvani's unfortunate frogs.

The middle is also a good place to check your use of detail, metaphor, and voice. Are you still using all the tools available to you? Are you using them with as much energy as you did at the outset? If not, take a break and recharge.

Bring it Home

The last segment of your essay may not be the easiest to write, but it's often the most exciting. As the internal and external journeys come to an end, the writer can take a long view of both, and the new perspective can be enlightening for both writer and reader.

You may refine and deepen the insights you had during your initial research, especially if you've turned up new material during the writing process. You may have an entirely different insight as you write. The new story you ultimately carry home may not be the one you expected to find.

This happens to me all the time: When I started to assess

the modern relevance of Aldo Leopold in a *High Country News* essay called "Where's Aldo?," I realized during the writing process that I needed to include the evolution of his views over his lifetime. When I set out to complain about the lack of a proper name for the wind in the Columbia River Gorge, the writing process led me to a literary reference to a nameless wind—"the secret wind of the desert." That gave my internal journey, and the resulting *Last Word on Nothing* essay, a fanciful new ending.

Remember that while writers tend to fuss over openings, endings are just as important, if not more so: They're your last words to your readers, and the ones they're most likely to remember. Endings serve as a sort of souvenir for the reader, a reminder of the external and internal journeys shared.

Essayists sometimes end by revealing (or reiterating) an insight from the journey:

> *The most temperamental piece of laboratory equipment will always be the human brain.* — George Johnson, "Millikan," in *The Ten Most Beautiful Experiments*

> *There is grandeur in this view of life, with its several powers, having been originally breathed by the Creator into a few forms or into one; and that, whilst this planet has gone cycling on according to the fixed law of gravity, from so simple a beginning endless forms most beautiful and most wonderful have been, and are being evolved.* — Charles Darwin, *On the Origin of Species*

They may refer implicitly to one of the essay's insights with a small, memorable scene:

Under the second A24 there was a dead mouse; under the third and fourth, nothing. Under the fifth were two ship rats, one freshly killed and the other just a clump of matted fur with a very long tail. — Elizabeth Kolbert, "The Big Kill"

This bird pauses, holding position not 30 feet over your head, like a kite on a short string. It seems unsure whether to take you for a pile of dead meat. And you are sitting quite still. The confusion is understandable. — David Quammen, "Yin and Yang in the Tularosa Basin," in *Natural Acts*

Or they may spell out an insight within a scene:

It seemed to me that if wild birds survive in modern Europe, it will be in the manner of those ancient small Franciscan buildings sheltered by the structures of a vain and powerful church: as beloved exceptions to the rule. — Jonathan Franzen, "Emptying the Skies"

Figarola told me that he loved his job because he and his staff are allowed to give care without measure—they can act on empathy. As Mathews worked, a little crescent of fingertip landed on the table between Figarola and me. "I work in utopia," he told me, and threw the scrap away with a bit of paper tissue. — Rebecca Solnit, "The Separating Sickness: How Leprosy Teaches Empathy"

A few weeks ago, in the country, far from the lights of the city, I saw the entire sky "powdered with stars" (in Milton's words); such a sky, I imagined, could be seen only on high, dry plateaus like that of Atacama in Chile (where some of the world's most powerful telescopes are). It was this celestial splendor that suddenly made me realize how little time, how little life, I had left. My sense of the heavens' beauty, of eternity, was inseparably mixed for me with a sense of transience—and death. — Oliver Sacks, "My Periodic Table"

Essays sometimes follow a classic feature-story structure by returning to the beginning at the end—by elaborating on or reconsidering a scene from the beginning of the essay, a strategy that often has the added benefit of contrasting the existing story with the new one. Contemporary essays frequently end with a coda—a short scene, like those quoted above, that in some way recalls the essay as a whole but can also stand on its own. Reported essays, which are often categorized as feature stories, can also close with a memorable quote from a source.

Ending a science essay can be particularly difficult, because in science, the end of one story is always the beginning of the next. And in essays, as in science, no conclusion is beyond doubt. But as many of the examples above show, it's possible to give the reader a sense of resolution without pretending to a final answer: You can pause along the path, and gesture ahead.

Write the First Draft

I haven't given you a lot of specific writing rules in this chapter. That's partly because, as I mentioned earlier, you can find a lot of very good basic writing advice elsewhere, and partly because the essay form has very few rules. This flexibility can be daunting, but take advantage of the opportunity to take chances: read a wide variety of good essays, like those referenced here, to give yourself a sense of the possibilities, and experiment at will, especially in your first draft. You'll have plenty of time during revisions to clean up any mishaps—and you just might discover something wonderful.

6 | Revising Essays

The secret to editing your work is simple: You need to become its reader instead of its writer.
— Zadie Smith, "That Crafty Feeling," in *Changing My Mind: Occasional Essays*

Writing is almost always a solitary process, but editing is not. That's fortunate for both writers and readers: Editors can see more clearly through readers' eyes, and by doing so can strengthen your connection to the reader. (Several sharp-eyed editors saved you from having to read the first draft of this book.) That said, writers can and should edit themselves as much as possible; the further you take a piece on your own, the happier you'll be with the final product.

In this chapter, I'll discuss how to edit your own drafts, and how to work with editors and fact-checkers to make your essays clear, readable, and accurate. I'll focus on the editing and revision strategies most applicable to essays; for more general advice, see the Resources & Further Reading section.

Get Some Distance

The best way to become a reader of your work instead of its writer, as Zadie Smith says above, is to get some distance from the page. Ideally, you'll be able to set your first draft aside for days or even weeks, returning to it with eyes that are as much like a reader's as possible. If you're on a tight deadline, try to build in some time, even if it's only an hour, to walk away from your draft. If you can only take a short break, use it to exercise a different part of your brain: Go for a run, play with your kids, cook a meal, watch a movie trailer. (Seriously—it helps!)

Whether or not you can take significant time off, there are other ways to gain distance. Printing out your draft can give you perspective on your writing, as can reading it aloud; if you trip over a phrase, your readers probably will, too. Even a change of location can help: When I need to get a fresh look at a draft, I sometimes take my laptop or a pile of pages to the coffee shop. The new scenery clears the mind, and the caffeine doesn't hurt, either.

Move From the Forest to the Trees

I'm a firm believer in working from macro to micro, in both writing and editing. Why worry about pronouns before your structure is settled? While it's tempting to fiddle with words during your first read—small tasks are less intimidating, after all—try to resist the urge.

On your first read, look for structural flaws. Do all your journeys, internal and external, have beginnings, middles, and ends? (Some segments may be implicit, which is fine.) Even a carefully outlined piece may be missing the ending or beginning of one of its journeys. I have a tendency to include *two* endings, which makes me sound like a party guest lingering at the door.

Tangled chronologies are another source of structural trouble. As I mentioned in Chapter 3, unless you have a very good reason to move back and forth in time (see *The Empathy Exams*) be kind to your readers and stick with a linear chronology. One of my favorite editors once sent me this tactful note: "The temporal structure of the story may be a bit too complex, since it starts 40 years ago, comes to the present, and steps back to 1857." Oops, I hadn't noticed that. The chronological complexity wasn't necessary, and it was easy to fix.

During this initial read, check the strength of your conclusions, too. If your essay makes an explicit argument, is it logical and solidly supported? Have you anticipated, considered, and responded to opposing views? If you spot large-scale problems, go back to the keyboard and fix them. If you can, take another break before returning to the draft for a second read.

This time, look for boring and confusing parts. If you rush impatiently through a paragraph, your reader will too. If at any point you have to reread your own writing to make sense of it, imagine how your reader will feel. Mark these spots, and then ask yourself:

Can you get rid of them? "Try to leave out the part readers tend to skip," advises novelist Elmore Leonard. Writers almost always lose perspective on what's important and what's not—that's one of the many reasons we all need editors—but you may have gained enough distance on your writing to see that a dull or confusing paragraph can be cut without compromising the piece's accuracy or integrity.

Can you shorten them? Is each sentence doing a unique job, or are you repeating yourself? Is your description excessive? "Decide what counts, what tells, and cut and recombine till what's left is what counts," writes novelist Ursula Le Guin. If you're a scientist writing about your own research, remember that it's possible to sacrifice precision without sacrificing accuracy, and that doing so often makes boring parts move faster and confusing parts read more clearly. Find the nerve to simplify.

Can you fix the boring parts by restoring your personal voice? Even though I've written essays for years, news voice still crops up in my drafts—usually in the middle, where my energy has flagged. Researchers often revert to passive voice, or to specialized vocabulary. When you spot these slips of voice, recall the imaginary individual reader I described in the previous chapter. How would you communicate this boring but necessary information to her or him? You'd drop the journalese or the technical language and talk like a normal person, right? Do that.

While you're at it, look for opportunities to use humor: A wry comment can instantly revive a weary reader. (David Quammen often uses funny asides when plowing through complicated or dull bits of background. "Whoa, if you're skimming, stop here," he says at one point in *The Song of the Dodo*.)

Can you fix the boring parts with a scene? Dull but necessary information can often be transmitted through a scene or anecdote, as George Johnson did in the section of "Galvani" quoted in the previous chapter. Remember that scenes can and should be used anywhere in an essay, not just at the beginning and the end.

Can you fix the confusing parts by improving the blocking? In Jenny Offill's novel *Dept. of Speculation*, a harried writing teacher flips out and begins writing the same thing on all of her students' stories: "WHERE ARE WE IN TIME AND SPACE? WHERE ARE WE IN TIME AND SPACE?" I laughed in recognition, and in sympathy for both teacher and writer. Because writers can so easily visualize the scenes they're describing, they frequently forget to "block" them for readers—to place characters and events in time and space, just as a playwright uses stage directions to position his or her performers. If you have to stop and reread a paragraph, check its blocking. Is it clear who's speaking, and where he or she is located? Are there lingering snarls in the chronology? Where are we in time and space?

After addressing the problems you find during your second read, you should have a fairly polished draft. If I have time at this point, I'll send my draft to an informal editor—a friend or colleague who can point out the big-picture problems I've missed. If I don't have time for an informal edit, I move straight on to my third read, when I finally let myself start fiddling.

The Third Read

During this read, focus on the sentence level and below. Pay special attention to:

Transitions. Do you trip up, mentally or verbally, as you move from one sentence to the next? Ann Finkbeiner, the former director of the graduate program in science writing at Johns Hopkins University, suggests smoothing transitions between sentences with what she calls the "AB/BC rule," where the end of a sentence is securely but almost invisibly linked to the beginning of the next. Here's an example from "In Darwin's Footsteps," a *New York Times* essay by Jonathan Weiner:

> *After several years of meticulous measurements, the Grants and their students realized that the finches' dimensions were changing before their eyes. Their beaks and bodies were evolving and adapting from year to year, sometimes slowly, sometimes strikingly, generation after generation.*

"Their beaks and bodies" refers to and elaborates upon "the finches' dimensions," tying the two sentences together without repeating words or using a standard conjunction.

Pronoun references. Blocking problems, mentioned above, are sometimes caused by vague or missing pronoun references. ("It" is by far the worst offender.) Make sure that each of your pronouns refers to a specific noun.

Clichés. Scour them out. No breakthroughs, please, and no Holy Grails.

Rhythm. The particular rhythm of your words and sentences is part of your personal voice, and most writers create it unconsciously. But it's often illuminating, at this stage of self-editing, to read your draft aloud with an ear to its rhythm: Are all your sentences the same length? How about your words? Do you favor short Germanic words, or long Latinate ones? (For general audiences, Germanic words should be your basic ingredients, and Latinate words the carefully employed spices.) If your rhythm sounds repetitive, you may be lulling your readers to sleep. Vary your sentence and word lengths and listen to the difference.

Verbs. While the evils of passive voice are sometimes greatly exaggerated (see what I did there?) it is wise to minimize your use of all forms of the verb "to be." Vivid, active verbs can enliven even long-past scenes: Recall the colonists who "stewed," "jellied," and "salted" pigeons in Chapter 4.

Emphasis. In general, the most memorable word in each sentence is the last one, so choose it deliberately. Consider the observation, attributed to Margaret Mead, that "fathers are biological necessities, but social accidents." What if Mead had reversed the phrases? "Fathers are social accidents, but biological necessities" means the same thing, but it's less provocative—and more forgettable.

Spelling and grammar. Use your word processor's spelling and grammar checker, of course, but don't forget to check by hand for commonly confused words (its/it's, your/you're, insure/ensure, loose/lose … know your bugbears). Yes, these are tiny problems, but do your editor a favor and fix them.

After tinkering with words and phrases to my obsessive-compulsive heart's content, I give my draft one last read and consider the essay as a whole. Does it still say what I want it to say? If so, it's time for my assigning editor to take a look.

Working with Essay Editors

For some excellent general advice on working with editors near and far, see Chapters 8 and 17 of *The Science Writers' Handbook*. Even if you're an experienced writer, one accustomed to and appreciative of the editing process, you may feel a twinge when your first essay edits appear in your inbox. Writers always put something of themselves into their stories, but essays are explicitly personal, and criticism can hurt. Remember that your editor is on your side; you're working together to make sure your ideas reach their audience. Remember, too, the dispassionate "view from the ceiling" that you've acquired over time and during the writing of your drafts.

Ideally, you'll go through two significant rounds with your editor, a structural edit and a more specific line edit. (The editing process is often a lot messier—this is human communication, after all—but in general, you and your editor should be moving from very broad to more specific concerns, as you did in your own readings of the draft.)

Once your assigning editor has signed off on the piece, he or she may send it to other editors on staff for review, or it may go directly to a copyeditor for a grammar and style check. Meanwhile, fact-checking will get underway.

Final Fact-checking

The first draft you submit to your assigning editor should be fact-checked, but after all of the additions, subtractions, and rearrangements of the editing process are complete, you should go through a final round of it. (If you're writing a personal essay, you should also pay one last visit to the ethical considerations outlined in Chapter 4.)

If you're writing for a major magazine, you'll probably work with a staff or freelance fact-checker. In most cases, he or she will request that you send a footnoted draft that lists your source or sources for every quote, fact, and general statement in the draft. When a checker questions your reporting, and good ones almost always do, don't take offense. You're both working toward the same goal, which is an accurate story.

I almost always create a footnoted draft whether or not I'm working with a fact-checker, since footnoting forces me to methodically re-confirm and update all my facts. While thorough fact-checking of any sort is a headache— I've described it elsewhere as "a particularly demented form of needlepoint"—it's always necessary, and often reassuring.

7 | Publishing Essays, Today & Tomorrow

It doesn't matter how obscure or arcane or esoteric your place of publication may be: Some sweet law ensures that the person who should be scrutinizing your work eventually does do so.
— Christopher Hitchens, *Hitch-22: A Memoir*

We're nearing the end of our journey through the essay form, and it's time to find an audience. Essays, after all, are containers for ideas, and they're only successful if the containers reach their intended recipients.

In this chapter, I'll look more closely at the current—and potential—audiences for essays in the digital age.

71

Essays are Everywhere

In Chapter 1, I mentioned that essays and essay elements can be found throughout modern media, from traditional op-ed pages to Facebook posts. I wasn't exaggerating. Opportunities to use your essay skills include:

Features and profiles. Many feature stories can be described as long, deeply reported essays, and feature writers often use a strong personal voice to narrate both their own journeys and those of their subjects. Most profile writers also use a personal voice, and profiles of well-known people often seek to overturn or deepen the existing story about their subject, returning from their journey with something new.

Multimedia. Many of the tales told by scientists and science journalists at The Story Collider's shows make literal use of personal voices to examine stories and draw broader relevance from them. Both the old and *Cosmos* series are, in a sense, extended essays enhanced by video and special effects. The wonderful paper-puppet animations produced by Flora Lichtman and Sharon Shattuck for *The New York Times* are essentially essays about science history, as is "The Fragile Framework," a comic about global climate negotiations created by Richard Monastersky and Nick Sousanis for the journal *Nature*.

Social media. Remember that tantalizing "turning in the head" that happens when an editor or writer hears a promising essay idea? When you promote your work on social media, you can create that same kind of curiosity in readers by posing a triggering question, beginning to recount a journey, or challenging an existing story. This can be done very straightforwardly: I once promoted an author interview I'd conducted for *National Geographic* by tweeting, "The story of Western #wildfire is not the one you think you know."

While I won't go so far as to say that a tweet can qualify as a full essay, other types of posts certainly can, and social media can instantly transport them to new audiences. Photographers frequently use Instagram captions, for instance, to describe the journey that led to the shot, or to reference a larger story represented by the image. Writer Brooke Jarvis introduced her *Harper's* story about Oregon end-of-life doctor Peter Rassmussen with a pair of Instagram images accompanied by a beautifully realized mini-essay.

In early January 2016, when *Baltimore Sun* staffer Adam Marton saw a list of the 344 homicide victims in his city during the previous year, one name caught his eye. In a public post on Facebook, Marton wrote:

Thelonious Monk, 28, was one of Baltimore's 344 homicide victims in 2015. A man named Thelonious Monk stole my car in August 2003. He fished my keys out of the night drop of an auto shop on Howard Street one summer night. It was barely an inconvenience, such is my life. Insurance covered a loaner and my wife and I went on vacation, as planned. When I got my car back a few weeks later, Thelonious had installed a baby seat and a subwoofer and the car was strewn with job applications. It was and remains one of the most heartbreaking scenes of my life. Our lives crossed, however oddly and briefly, and I can't help but think that Thelonious probably never had a chance. A chance to escape, a chance to succeed. The opportunities I have always enjoyed. I suspect that the man murdered in Baltimore this year is the same young man that stole my car 12 years ago. I feel like maybe he was trying to use my car to make a break for it. I wish he had made it. Rest in peace, young man, I will never forget you.

Marton expanded on the story in a *Sun* column a few days later. But his brief post, which went viral and drew national news attention, had already done everything an essay should.

Finding Publishers

Publishing could have been one of the first sections of this book, not one of the last: Each publication has its distinctive style and sensibility, and it's often easier to develop essay ideas and write a draft when you have particular outlets and readers in mind. But I think it's even more important to know and practice—not to mention enjoy—the craft before you start looking for an audience.

Since the markets for essays are changing as quickly as the rest of the proverbial media landscape, I'll focus on types of publications rather than specific titles, and follow the list with some general advice on pitching. Note that though many outlets publish essays, very few use the term. Look for section names such as "Comment," "Opinion," "Perspective," "Views," and "First Person."

Newspapers, small and large. Major newspapers such as *The New York Times* and *The Washington Post* have a large and growing appetite for essays of all kinds. Traditionally, essays and other opinion pieces were confined to a single page opposite the newspaper's own editorial ("op-ed" is short for "opposite editorial"), but the popularity of essays in the digital age has greatly expanded their territory. Regional and local newspapers are also recognizing the value of essays from outside contributors, and alternative weeklies are especially welcoming.

Magazines, ditto. Many magazines have dedicated essay pages in their print editions, and many publish additional essays online. But don't limit your scope to essay sections: Your idea might work best as a feature, a profile, or a book review. Maybe you can turn it into a service piece for a health or other consumer magazine. Think broadly.

Digital-only publications. The division between newspapers and magazines is fading, and many digital publications combine elements of both, frequently experimenting with different formats and approaches. *Slate* and *Vox*, for example, cover breaking news but also use first-person pieces throughout their sites, and look for writers with strong personal voices. Large digital publications generally pay less than print magazines, but as much or more than print newspapers.

Scientific journals. Most journals publish essays, often in the form of expert commentaries. These are excellent places for scientists to reach the wider scientific community, connecting issues in their area of expertise with broad trends in science or policy. Some journals also use essays to commemorate important scientific discoveries and other events. (If your essay is tied to an anniversary, be sure to submit it for consideration well before the date in question.)

Blogs. Blogs aren't so much a type of publication as a publishing tool—"blog" is about as descriptive as "paper and ink"—and blogs range from extremely professional, well-staffed commercial operations (*Slate* and *Vox* are essentially multi-channel blogs) to one-person labors of love. Many science blogs are written by individuals or small groups but formally associated with magazines, such as the *Phenomena* blogs at *National Geographic* and the blogs within the *Scientific American* blog network. *The Last Word on Nothing*, which I write for regularly, is an independent group blog. Most blogs are open to guest posts, but many do not pay contributors.

Literary magazines. Literary magazines are the place to find readers—and editors—who prize essays for their own sake, rather than as news commentaries or feature stories. Essays in literary magazines are often lengthy, and may be deeply reported. Writers can expect intelligent editing, small but discerning audiences, and low pay. (For an introduction to the literary-magazine scene, explore the online database assembled by Poets & Writers magazine.)

Pitching Essays

Before contacting a publication, familiarize yourself with its recent issues or posts. Make sure the submission you're considering fits the publication's style and interests, and doesn't overlap with recent stories.

Most newspapers, magazines, large digital publications, scientific journals, and literary magazines post submission guidelines on their sites, or will send guidelines on request. (The submission process for smaller blogs is usually much less formal; if there are no guidelines on the site, ask one of the blog's writers if he or she accepts guest posts.)

In general, editors will want to see a full draft before accepting a piece, because so much of the success of an essay depends on its voice and overall execution. News and feature editors, on the other hand, usually assign stories based on pitches; see Chapter 3 of *The Science Writers' Handbook* for more on the art of pitching.

Avoid sending your submission to a generic email such as "opinion@washingtonpost.com." Search the staff listings for a specific name and email, or ask friends and colleagues to recommend an editor. If your colleague knows one well, he or she may also be willing to introduce you, but don't use that colleague's name without permission. Return these favors—the mutually beneficial exchange of editor intel is a long-standing tradition among professional writers.

While an editor is unlikely to assign an essay based on a pitch, you can gauge his or her general interest in an idea before you start writing, especially if you already know or have written for the editor. Heather Abel, who wrote the "How to Stop a Tsunami in Three Easy Steps" essay described in Chapter 2, approached me with a short e-mail:

> *I'm thinking of writing an open letter to the children of the Pacific Northwest from a child of Southern California about earthquakes and tidal waves. I grew up absolutely terrified of a post-earthquake tsunami in Los Angeles.*

Stephen Ornes, who wrote "Archimedes in the Fence," said simply, "I'm writing an essay about the tragic nature of carpenter bees, and how I think of them as modern incarnations of Archimedes. I'm looking for a home for it."

As I mentioned in Chapter 2, I already knew and respected these writers' voices, and I thought that both ideas had great potential as essays. So it was easy for me to say "Yes, please go for it!"—with the understanding that I could only give a final answer after reading a completed draft. In other cases, these sorts of preliminary pitches have allowed me to warn writers when a similar essay is already in the works, or to suggest approaches most likely to work for a publication, saving both of us time and trouble.

Rejections of both pitches and drafts are common, but don't take them as a general judgment of your skills; they're almost always the result of a mismatch between piece and publication.

Once a newspaper, magazine, journal, or literary magazine has accepted your essay, you will likely be offered a fee and asked to sign a contract. (See Chapter 22 of *The Science Writers' Handbook* for more on negotiating fees and contracts.) While writing is a skill that should always be compensated, essay writers, in particular, are often asked to work for free. If you are an expert writing to promote an idea, or if you are a beginning writer in search of your first bylines, it may make sense for you to work solely for exposure, but do consider the tradeoffs. As an established professional writer, I write for free only when the creative satisfaction is irresistible—as it is at *The Last Word on Nothing*—or when I'm explicitly donating my work to a cause I support.

In traditional reporting, writers with a personal or financial stake in a subject are forbidden to write about it. In essay writing, however, writers have a personal stake in their subjects almost by definition. Such connections—personal, professional, financial, or otherwise—should be stated within the essay, or in a bio line at the end of the piece. If you have a stake that's not clearly explained in this way, be sure to tell your editor. If you're unsure whether it's important enough to disclose, err on the side of transparency. (For more on conflicts of interest, see Chapter 23 of *The Science Writers' Handbook*.)

Final Thoughts

We started this journey with Eula Biss, who contemplated the bitter cultural standoff over vaccines and wondered if, instead of portraying the debate as a battle between education and ignorance, we could "accept a world in which we are all irrational rationalists."

For those of us who love and respect the scientific process, this may sound like heresy. We don't need *irrational* rationality—we need rational rationality! For many years, science communicators have tried to translate scientific findings for popular audiences, trusting that once people understand the facts, they will make rational decisions based on those facts. But this model of communication—sometimes called the "information-deficit model"—simply isn't enough.

No matter our profession or level of education, our decisions are driven by a combination of instinct and reason, with reason often serving to justify our initial instinctive response. We need reason, but we need instinct, too: Psychologists have found that when our instinctive abilities are damaged, we are overwhelmed by apparently identical choices and become unable to make decisions at all.

Facts matter. Science matters. But in order to effectively communicate scientific findings, we have to consider both the people who produce them and the people who apply them—and all of those people are, as Biss puts it, "irrational rationalists," influenced by facts *and* by a welter of instincts and emotions. As science writers, we can't just insist that people act more rationally: We have to meet them where they are, which happens to be where we are, too.

I believe that essays are one way to do this. Essays allow writers to not only explain the facts but also explore the complicated process by which knowledge is created and spread, observing how reason and instinct operate within us all. By doing so, essays help us see science and ourselves more clearly—and better understand the flaws and the beauty in both.

Resources & Further Reading

All of the essays quoted in the text can be found online or in widely available books.

Essay Anthologies and Collections

The Art of the Personal Essay: An Anthology from the Classical Era to the Present, edited by Phillip Lopate, is the definitive personal-essay anthology.

Essayists on the Essay: Montaigne to Our Time, edited by Carl Klaus and Ned Stuckey-French, is a collection of short essays by essayists about their chosen form.

The Best American Essays anthologies, published annually, are almost always excellent and diverse selections of current essays.

The Best American Science and Nature Writing anthologies often include essays.

The Best American Essays of the Century, edited by Joyce Carol Oates, is a terrific core sample of 20th-century essays.

Great Essays in Science, edited by Martin Gardner, is very stale, pale, and male, but it does include a fine selection of pre-twentieth-century science essays.

At Large and At Small: Familiar Essays, by Anne Fadiman, is both a lovely collection of essays and a meditation on the essay form itself.

General Writing Advice

After more than 50 years as a near-sacred text, *The Elements of Style*, by William Strunk and E.B. White, has accumulated a few critics, but there's still no pithier introduction to the art of writing.

On Writing Well, by William Zinsser, is a classic guide by a master teacher.

On Writing: A Memoir of the Craft, by Stephen King, is part memoir, part no-nonsense writing guide.

Steering the Craft: A Twenty-first Century Guide to Sailing the Sea of Story, by Ursula Le Guin, is aimed at fiction writers, but its insights are useful to nonfiction writers, too.

Ben Yagoda's *The Sound on the Page: Style and Voice in Writing* is an illuminating consideration of the elusive concept of voice.

Telling True Stories, edited by Mark Kramer and Wendy Call, is an idiosyncratic collection of advice from many of the best nonfiction writers working today.

Journalist and journalism teacher Jacqui Banaszynski has posted an assortment of useful handouts and other materials on her website, jacquibanaszynski.com.

Science Writing and Science Communication

The Science Writers' Handbook. What are you waiting for?

Escape from the Ivory Tower: A Guide to Making Your Science Matter, by Nancy Baron, is an excellent guide for academics and other experts interested in communicating with broader audiences.

Science Blogging: The Essential Guide, edited by Christie Wilcox, Bethany Brookshire, and Jason Goldman, is a how-to manual for communicating scientific research online.

Communicating Popular Science: From Deficit to Democracy, by Sarah Tinker Perrault, is an insightful study of the strengths and shortfalls of modern science communication.

Ethics and Fact-checking

While you should always consult your assigning editor (and your own gut) about ethical dilemmas, the *New York Times* ethics handbook, available online, is a useful summary of standard practices.

The Fact Checker's Bible: A Guide to Getting it Right, by Sarah Harrison Smith, is a good overview of standard fact-checking practices at major magazines.

Acknowledgements

Thanks to the board, staff, and membership of the National Association of Science Writers for the Idea Grant that made this project possible.

I'm grateful to all the members of SciLance, who brought the original *Handbook* into being and assisted with this companion book in many small and large ways. Particular thanks to Monya Baker, who served as my editor throughout the project, and Stephen Ornes, who was a perceptive reader and commenter.

Thanks to Rob Irion, Ann Finkbeiner, and Sarah Rabkin for so generously sharing their time and pedagogical wisdom.

Thanks also to copyeditor *extraordinaire* Diane Sylvain, who made sure that "lightsaber" was one word and that Montaigne wore a ruffled collar, not a powdered wig.

Finally, deep bows of gratitude to all the editors, fellow writers, family members, and friends with whom I've discussed these ideas over the years. Writing is a solitary business—but not, thanks to you, a lonely one.

About the Author

Michelle Nijhuis is a regular contributor to *National Geographic*, *The New Yorker*'s science-and-tech blog *Elements*, and other publications. She is also the longtime editor of the essay section of *High Country News*, a magazine known for its coverage of science and natural resource issues in the American West. Her reported essays and feature stories—which examine subjects ranging from caviar smuggling in the Ozarks to life off the electrical grid to her daughter's conviction that Bilbo Baggins is a girl—have been recognized with several national awards and included in three *Best American* anthologies. With Thomas Hayden, she is the co-editor of *The Science Writers' Handbook: Everything You Need to Know to Pitch, Publish, and Prosper in the Digital Age*. She lives with her family in rural Washington state.

Printed in the USA
CPSIA information can be obtained
at www.ICGtesting.com
LVHW101827180823
755638LV00003B/389